Michael Hilscher, Ph.D

Blake the Drake

and the Enchanting Egg

Illustrations by Laura Ullrich

For my daughter, Mia. I love you!
Your Papa

Blake the Drake,
the nicest drake at the pond,
sat ever so sadly in front of his empty nest.

He sighed. "I wish I had an egg in my nest.
I would be so wonderful to be a papa duck.
If I had one wish, it would be to have a baby duckling of
my very own to raise and love."

Darcy Duck, the sweetest duck at the pond, overheard him and wanted ever so badly to help Blake the Drake feel better. She felt sorry for him, because she herself had lots of eggs in her nest but Blake the Drake didn't have any. That's when Darcy Duck had a wonderful idea.

Blake the Drake was so happy
he did a somersault and said to Darcy:
"You would really do that for me? Are you sure?
That would be the nicest thing anyone has ever
done for me."

Darcy Duck replied: "Yes, I'm very sure. I love all of my eggs, but I know that once your baby duckling hatches and you raise it and give it all your love, it will have the very best life any baby duckling could ask for. It will be the most loved duckling in the whole pond.
I know you'll be the most loving, most caring papa duck ever, because you want your baby duckling so very badly."
Then Darcy Duck carefully removed an egg from her nest and gently placed it in Blake the Drake's nest. It was a most enchanting egg.

"Oh, thank you, Darcy Duck. I'll never forget you.
You made my lifelong dream come true."

Blake the Drake was over the moon.
He loved the egg
more than anything else in all the world.
He sat down on the egg
as quickly as he could
and began to wait,
and wait, and wait...

He sat on the egg day and night,
but the duckling just wouldn't hatch.

Blake became very sad,
but he stayed put to make sure
the egg was nice and warm.
He didn't give up because
he wanted a duckling
so badly.

One day, Ducky Diana,
the friendliest duck at the pond,
happened to stroll by Blake's nest and
saw him crying.

Ducky Diana said:
"Why are you crying?"

to which Blake the Drake replied:
"Darcy Duck gave me one of her eggs and
I love it more than anything.
My greatest wish in the whole wide world
is to become a papa duck and
to love and raise my baby duck.
I've been sitting here on the egg day and night,
but my duckling still hasn't hatched."

Ducky Diana chuckled and said:
"Blake, you silly drake, don't you know
that papa ducks can't make baby ducks hatch?
Only mama ducks can do that."

Ducky Diana smiled and said to Blake the Drake: "Don't be sad, dear Blake. We can fix this. I'm a mama duck, you know. I'd love to help you make your dream come true. If you like, I will hatch your egg for you. And when your duckling is born, you can finally be a papa duck."

Ducky Diana got right to work.
    She sat down on the egg and began to wait.

    Blake the Drake was very excited and
stayed right by Diana's side.

    Every hour, he would ask:
    "Diana, has my duckling hatched yet?"
    and each time, Diana would answer:
    "Not yet, Blake. Patience."

"Blake, I think it's time.
Your duckling is hatching."

Bursting with excitement and curiosity, Diana and Blake stood by the egg and watched as the shell began to crack open.

As soon as the duckling's head appeared, Blake said to Diana:
"I'm the happiest papa duck in the whole wide world.
Thank you, Diana, I'll never forget you and Darcy
for helping my dream come true."

Blake turned back to his baby duckling, and with tears in his eyes,
wrapped his wings around his duckling, and said:

"I LOVE YOU MORE THAN ANYTHING
IN THE WORLD. I'LL KEEP YOU SAFE YOUR
WHOLE LIFE LONG, AND I'LL ALWAYS
BE HERE FOR YOU."

The baby duckling looked deep into Blake's eyes
and loudly quacked,

Blake the Drake laughed as tears of joy rolled down his beak.
He said:
"And that's exactly what I'll call you,
Mia. Mia the Duck."

From that moment on, the two were inseparable.
All of the ducks from the pond came together
for a big party to celebrate
Mia the Duck and Blake the Drake's happiness.
Mia and Blake were the luckiest
duck familythe pond had ever seen.

Blake the Drake and Me

The idea for this book was inspired by true events, namely my own personal story about fulfilling my greatest wish of becoming a father.

For as long as I can remember, I have wanted to have children. I couldn't imagine not starting a family of my own. But there's one small stumbling block. I'm gay. After giving it much thought and consideration and dredging my way through some deep moments of despair, I found a solution that felt right. An egg donor and a surrogate mother overseas both stepped up to help me fulfil my heart's desire. In 2015, I held my beautiful Mia for the first time in my arms!

When Mia was old enough to ask about the circumstances surrounding her birth, I used the metaphor of a magical egg that someone else had hatched to explain how she arrived on our planet. This was my way of sharing her story in a child-friendly, truthful, and plausible manner. And that's how the story of Blake the Drake came about. This book is close to my heart. I hope to offer encouragement to others in a similar situation and to show people that you can achieve anything once you set your mind to it. But above all, this book is for every child who has come into the world in this way, who is living in a "new" family structure. I hope to show them—through a loving and captivating story—how much they are wanted and loved.

Michael Hilscher, Ph.D

Text and storyline: Michael Hilscher, Ph.D
Illustrator: Laura Ullrich (UllrichArt)
Translation: Cynthia Pecking,
Editing: Don Henderson

This book belongs to:

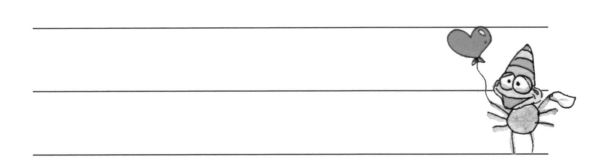